HABITS
4
MIRACLES

Design Your Life Your Way

RAHUL KARAN SHARMA

Absolute Author
Publishing House

Habits4Miracles
Copyright © 2023 RAHUL KARAN SHARMA

Publisher: Absolute Author Publishing House

Editor: Dr. Melissa Caudle

ISBN:978-1-64953-701-0

In the loving memory of my vibrant brother, Parag Karan Sharma, your spirit continues to touch my life daily. Though your physical presence is no longer with us, the love, laughter, and memories you shared remain deeply rooted in our hearts.

As I watch Yuvaan grow, his exuberance and joy remind me of the light you brought into our lives. No one can fill the void of your absence but the happiness and warmth he brings help ease the pain of your loss.

Forever in my heart, I love you Bhai.

Dedication

This book is devoted to those who persevere and choose to try again. In the ever-unfolding story of our lives, we face countless decisions every day. Some decisions may lead to less-than-ideal outcomes, while others bring about significant, positive changes.

This moment, this book, this transformative journey, is for you. Regardless of your identity or circumstances, let me guide you in reshaping the course of your life by unveiling the incredible power of your mind to manifest miracles. Embrace the opportunity for profound transformation. You, my friend, are truly deserving of all the MIRACLES that await you.

Gratitude

I am immensely grateful to my loving wife, Parul, and kids Kaina and Yuvaan for their love and support, which gave me the strength to complete this book. Their unwavering encouragement and faith in me made a world of difference.

To my dear parents, words cannot express my gratitude for everything you have done to mold me into the person I am today. Your selfless sacrifices and relentless efforts have never gone unnoticed, and I will always be indebted to your boundless love and support.

My mentor and coach, Dr. Delatorro McNeal, I am truly humbled and grateful for your shared wisdom and motivation. You helped unveil the writer within me and equipped me with the tools to thrive. THANK YOU!

Recognizing the Influence of Positive Change: Reviews for Habits4MIRACLES

"Every one of us is nothing more than the sum total of what we truly believe about ourselves. What we believe results in our habits and if we change our habits, we change our lives. Rahul Sharma has broken down this process into immediately actionable steps that can be applied to your life. Each chapter will take you step by step into the life you've always wanted. Rahul has always been hungry for personal growth and this book will help you in your personal growth journey, too!"

Ken Hartley
International Keynote Speaker, Best-Selling Author of *God Wired* and *Leadership Illusions*

"Rahul Sharma's wisdom and practical, real-world advice will truly make a positive difference in your life. If you're serious about growth and creating life changing habits, invest in this book today."

Waldo Waldman
Author of the New York Times & Wall Street Journal Bestseller *Never Fly Solo*

"This is an extremely practical and actionable book. Rahul has tested these strategies in his own life and created a logical, step-by-step process to help you inculcate the most life-changing habits in your life. These easy to implement concepts can lead you towards a truly miraculous life."

Nishant Kapoor
Productivity Coach at Nerd Productivity

"This book has significantly helped me change my daily routine, and I already see the benefits. One of my favorite insights from the book is the concept of 'mind talk' and how it can help us design our lives."

Sanjeev Gupta
Entrepreneur

"I usually read 100+ books yearly so know a good one when I read it. What I love about Habits4Miracles is that the fluff is removed, and the author is not using techniques to fill the pages. What you get is very valuable information that you can start using immediately to improve your life."

Roy Coughlan DTM PMP
Podcast Coach and Host of 5 Successful Podcasts

"'Habits 4 Miracles' by Rahul Sharma gives straightforward, straight-to-the point guidance on how to optimally use your mindset. He also gives practical tools at the end of each chapter so that you can start implementing them in your life. This book will help you understand your inner power and how best to use it to achieve desired results."

Roberta Ndlela
Podcast Host and Soft Skills Trainer

"Habits determine our future. That's why books like Habits4miracles are important. With insightful and actionable strategies, this book is a valuable resource for advancing one's personal or professional life."

SCAN ME

Ryan Jenkins, CSP
Wall Street Journal Bestselling Author of *Connectable: How Leaders Move Teams From Isolated to All In*

"Habits4Miracles is a blend of anecdotal and scientific evidence that makes for a compelling and informative read, while also providing actionable advice for readers. Rahul's ability to draw from personal experiences and use research to support his ideas is also praiseworthy. The use of mindful strategies and purposes, along with call to actions, adds another layer of depth to his book. "Habits4Miracles" is a valuable resource for anyone looking to improve their habits and achieve their goals."

SCAN ME

Olga Nikitidou Rosenberg
Coach for a positive mind and body

"In a world full of self-help books filled with empty promises and shallow advice, Habits4Miracles stands out as a powerful and engaging guide to personal growth and success. But the carefully curated "Call to Action" exercises truly set Habits4Miracles apart. These transformative steps will lead you from a world of aspirations to a life of dreams actualized. Don't settle for just dreaming about your potential; embrace the M.I.R.A.C.L.E.S. journey and start living it with Habits4Miracles."

Janet Macaluso
Founder, Learning2LEAD

"Rahul's book is the encouragement that we all need. Mindset can make a tremendous difference in our mental health and his evidence-based perspective gives us the grounding tools that we all need to feel better."

Dr. Lauren Cook
Clinical Psychologist and Author of Generation Anxiety

"I have always been interested in personal growth and development but needed help figuring out where to start. That is until I stumbled upon 'Habits4Miracles' by Rahul

Karan Sharma. One of the things I loved about the book was its practicality and action orientation. The author's writing is easy to understand, making it accessible to anyone, regardless of their experience with personal development."

Lavanya Khanna
Student, Rutgers School of Business

"Habits4Miracles is a refreshingly introspective, yet practical guide in how to design and live your best life through positive mind talk, mental discipline, and consistent positivity. Rahul writes in a personable, inspirational, and practical way so the reader immediately resonates on a mental, emotional, and spiritual level. This is a great read for anyone on the journey to designing the life they always wanted or wondering what it takes to live a life of peace, confidence, truth, and happiness."

Dr. Shirley Davis – Global Workforce & DEI Expert, Keynote Speaker, Bestselling Author of *Living Beyond "What If?" Release the Limits and Realize Your Dreams*

FOREWORD

As a Peak Performance Expert, one thing I constantly teach on and talk about is the power, capability, and influence of our mind. If we could realize the potential of our thoughts, we would be more intentional about what we gravitate to and what we accomplish. Most people use the smallest percentage possible of their brain cells, not recognizing that there is function and efficacy beyond the norm. There is brilliance beyond the routine. There is a greater manifestation of success beyond the basic usual. And it matters not what you desire to do in life or where you aspire to go; your mind matters. What you tell yourself matters. How you gravitate to and incorporate habits matters!

One of the scintillating effects of this book is that it tackles the power of the mind with such simplistic authority. Daily, we talk and think and recite. We direct, project, and prepare. However, one element we lack action in is respecting and appreciating the processes of our mental conversations that lead to better health and wellness in totality. This book will allow you to recognize that the highest levels of accomplishment, ascendancy, and dominance will take place once you implement this singular concept: appreciate the habits of the mind that birth the miracles of your life.

Dr. Delatorro L. McNeal, II, MSP, CSP
Wall Street Journal and USA Today
Bestselling Author of *Shift Into A Higher Gear: Better Your Best and Live Life to the Fullest*

Table of Contents

CHAPTER 7

CHAPTER 8

CONCLUSION

"If you pick the right small behavior and sequence it right, then you won't have to motivate yourself to have it grow. It will just happen naturally, like a good seed planted in a good spot." – BJ Fogg

PRELUDE

Introduction to *M.I.R.A.C.L.E.S.*

As we begin this journey, let us take a moment and consider habits. You know, those acquired behavior patterns that become involuntary. We all have them and often don't recognize their habitualness. Take a moment and think about your current habits, or even consider former habits that you have ceased to continue. Take inventory of whether you find (or found) them exciting. After consideration, you discover that what you envision will fall into two categories:

(1) *things that make you better,* or
(2) *things that make you worse.*

There is also the possibility you are considering adopting some new habits in your life. Depending on where you are in your life and where you desire to be, there may be a need for some new behaviors to adopt and adapt to. Even now, you might ask, "What exactly are new habits?"

Well, let's consider when people say that we must include greens in our diet each day. Not only is it about the benefits of vegetables, but it is also about the habit, the genuine concerted effort, of living a better and healthier lifestyle. We all understand the need to inculcate good habits. Habits are a part of life, absolutely. They must, however, bring positive change and growth into our lives. Sometimes we even proclaim just how necessary those "good" habits are. But the real question to ask ourselves is, "Are you finally ready to do something about it?"

If you answered "yes" to that question, I might be able to help you. What I bring to the table are vital and proven tools for success that have helped me over the years. These tools are not based on guesswork, but on solid wisdom and sound principles. I am not sharing anything I have not implemented and gained success from with you.

When it comes to habits, let us first be sure we have the proper definition. We know and understand what a habit is at first glance or initial hearing of the word. However, the definitive terms and phrases correlating with habits are acquired behavior patterns, customary practices, addictions, and obsessions. While the word "habit" may often have negative connotations attached, good habits exist. When implemented correctly, these habits are beneficial, healthy, and able to introspect one's life from the inside out.

Now, if we may, let's travel back in time, shall we? I want to share a personal story with you. When I implemented swimming into my fitness lifestyle two years ago, I was very eager to reconnect with an activity I first loved as a child. The pool at my gym had a 25-meter lap, and I knew nothing could stop me.

However, the first day of getting back into that routine was surprisingly tough. Even one lap felt challenging, and I had to take regular breaks before the second and third laps.

To make matters worse, I was dead tired by the end of the fourth lap. That just didn't make sense to me. To have the love for swimming I had, something was not adding up for me. Then it hit me; I was out of practice, for sure.

While I loved it in my early years, it was no longer a habit that I engaged in, and my body was no longer familiar with the act and the art of swimming. Mentally, I thought that I was ready. Physically, that's another story. On my way home, I engaged in my usual mind talk to figure out what had gone wrong. I considered a few options and studied more about swimming to be better equipped next time. I prepared myself through more mind talk and set a goal of eight laps without stopping.

It may have seemed unrealistic when I wrote it down and read it back to myself. However, I did not give up, and I did it. I stuck with it and gradually increased my completed number of laps. At one point, in just three weeks from setting the goal, I could even swim for forty whole laps – without stopping! This was a small instance of success because of the healthy habits that I developed over time. And yes, the "Not Giving Up" mindset will help you navigate more pressing life matters and decisions.

Ask yourself, "Why is it more reasonable and seemingly more doable to acquire the habit of something you dislike vs. establishing a positive routine of something you need?"

If you ponder, it always seems easier to do what we don't need to do than embrace what's necessary? With this in mind, we must recognize and remember that it takes a lot to build something concrete. Yes, it takes persistence and dedication to finish what you start and finish strong. That is why I want to share eight amazing tools that will aid you in your journey to consistency and positive behavior creation.

The eight tools discussed in this book, which I have practiced over the years and are referred to as *Habits4MIRACLES*, have enabled me to declutter my brain and identify workable solutions to situational problems.

This is not a game, and they sincerely work; you just have to do your part and work them. Now, I cannot force you to embrace the change you need, and I cannot demand you use this resource for your benefit. I can say that you will be glad you did if you choose to take this journey.

Sure, you can choose to use this book as a source of information about something new, or you can become more proactive by engaging with the calls to action after each chapter in the book. The choice is yours, but I can guarantee you that beginning with positive habits will start right here – reading this book and practicing the principles given.

Let's start rolling; our habits are shifting. If you are ready for the change you need, which I know you are, I'd like to welcome you to another era in your life and decision-making.

Without any delay, let me introduce you to the eight tools I regularly rely on. They are easy to remember, as I will introduce them using the acronym "M.I.R.A.C.L.E.S." as a cue in an autocratic approach.

SCAN ME   Scan now to become a member of our exclusive Habits4MIRACLES Facebook page community and contribute to the spread of happiness and positivity.

"None can destroy iron, but it's
rust can. Likewise, none can
destroy a person; but his own
mindset can." - Ratan Tata

CHAPTER 1

Untying the Knot <u>M</u> *"Mind Talk"*

Think for a moment about the things you have told yourself just today. Really consider the inner conversations you have had *with* you *about* you. Consider how those internal conversations made you feel and reflect on how you felt after the internal dialogue was over. This inner dialogue, known as "mind talk," is impacted by your subconscious mind and reveals your ideas, questions, and belief systems.

While you might not be conscious of it, you will likely participate. Positive mind-talk is essentially the key differentiator between success and failure. Did you know that?

Commonly referred to as self-talk, it rewires our brains to stay in a positive frame of mind. Therefore, your internal dialogue can be constructive or destructive, affecting how you feel about yourself and react to life's events.

According to studies, the act of merely reminiscing about a happy occasion can prolong emotions of happiness and lessen anxiety. Our subconscious mind has a hard time distinguishing between reality and imagination. Reliving those moments in our minds can make them feel just as authentic at the moment as they did during the moment they occurred.

Additionally, studies have indicated that those who refer to themselves by name rather than using the pronoun "I" during the process exhibit higher self-assurance and self-esteem. A team led by Ethan Kross of the University of Michigan evaluated the performance and stress levels of people about to deliver a speech to others. The participants were placed into two groups:

Group A - were instructed to speak to themselves in the first person.

Group B – were instructed to use third-person pronouns of their names.

It turns out that *Group B* fared much better than *Group A*. The results showed that even for susceptible people, the slightest changes in language used have a substantial impact. It directly affects their capacity to control their thoughts, feelings, and actions under stressful circumstances.

A man named John is feeling upset after a recent breakup. When John reflects on his feelings in the third person by asking, "Why is John upset?" he experiences less emotional reactivity compared to when he addresses himself in the first person by asking, "Why am I upset?" According to Jason Moser, an associate professor of psychology at Michigan State University, referring to oneself in the third person causes people to think about themselves in a similar way to how they think about others. This can help individuals achieve some psychological distance from their experiences, which can be helpful in regulating emotions. The study, which was partly funded by the National Institutes of Health and the John Temple Foundation, consisted of two experiments that strongly supported this primary conclusion.

Unleashing Your Mind's Superpower

The greatest gift nature has given to us is our mind. To unleash the tremendous power reserves which currently sleep within you, it is critical that you first become aware of the nature of the mind. According to Robin Sharma, Canadian author, leadership expert, and motivational speaker, the first step to successful living is to learn how to run your mind like a winner. The second step is to understand once and for all that your mind can create magic in your life if you only let it.

You are the only one who can set limitations in your life. When you think beyond limits and dream big, amazing things can happen, unleashing powerful forces that propel you forward. Robin also talks about the 10 Golden Rules for Mental Mastery in his book *Mega Living* which are:

1. The level of success is determined by what you think every second of every minute of every day.
2. Your outer world reflects your inner world. If you want to change your life, you must start by changing the thoughts you put into your mind.
3. You alone are responsible for what you think.
4. A super successful mindset does not happen in a day; you must work hard.
5. One of the great keys to a better life is to change your self-image.
6. Anything you faithfully and honestly believe you can achieve; you will achieve if you take persistent action in that

direction.

7. The Law of Attraction is the dominant law of the mind.
8. Your subconscious mind plays a particularly great role in the outcome of your life.
9. Your mind has the capacity to hold only one thought in its focus at any one time.
10. There is a Success Mechanism inside your mind that craves positive stimulation.

Do any of these Golden Rules resonate with you? I encourage you to revisit them and create a list of two to three action items that will aid you in designing your life your way.

Allow me to share a personal story from my college years when I began smoking. My roommate landed a job collaborating with and promoting a newly launched and famous cigarette brand. He had many packs available, and one of those two voices in my head made me cave in.

After a while, I felt that smoking impacted my health greatly, and I had to stop. I tried to trick myself into quitting this habit for almost a year through many techniques. I would do my best to remove cigarettes from around me or simply to not buy them anymore. I also tried other ways to stop but could only resist them for so long.

I finally engaged in some inner dialogue and went to a temple, asking God to grant me the strength to break the habit. I think it was the 27th of March in 2011 when I smoked my last cigarette. That experience alone made me believe in mind talk. It made me believe that if I could do it once, I could do it again. The situation did not matter to me. I knew I could overcome anything with this mind talk. Smoking is an issue that I feel many people struggle and battle with. However, with positive mind talk, you can definitely quit it.

There are two voices in your head. It doesn't matter what you label them or if you call them good and evil, yin and yang, or the devil and the angel. One leads you in the right direction, and the other leads you toward the wrong path. No matter how you spin it, those two voices are *you*. They represent the two sides of you: your conscience and the side filled with your desires.

Have you ever been in a dilemma where you had to make a difficult choice about whether or not to treat yourself to dessert after dinner? One voice told you not to indulge since you exercised more and met a weight loss goal. The other voice told you that indulging was okay because you only live once. Having a dessert after dinner may not seem like a huge decision. Still, you should remember that the accumulation of similar days works as a huge differentiator.

Think about it! The collection of those days distracts you from the plan you made for yourself. It was you who made the plan willingly. Therefore, why is it so difficult to stick to? Choosing your actions and sticking with them requires you to be mentally strong.

And yes, this is possible for anyone through mind talk.

Circle of Happiness

The Circle of Happiness is a holistic approach to achieving a more fulfilling, joyful, and well-rounded life. It is comprised of several interconnected elements that work together to cultivate a positive mindset and, ultimately, a positive and happier existence. These elements include:

1. Positive Mind Talk:
   - Use affirmations and positive mind-talk to boost your confidence and self-esteem.
   - Be compassionate towards yourself and acknowledge your progress and achievements.
   - Replace self-critical thoughts with

encouraging and supportive statements.

2. Positive Mindset:
   - Cultivate optimism and focus on the brighter aspects of situations.
   - Practice gratitude and appreciate the small things in life.
   - Embrace challenges as opportunities for growth and learning.

3. Positive Thoughts:
   - Engage in self-reflection and reframe negative thought patterns.
   - Surround yourself with positive influences, such as uplifting books, music, and people.
   - Practice mindfulness and meditation to stay present and aware of your thoughts.

4. Positive Actions:
   - Set achievable goals and take small, consistent steps towards them.
   - Engage in acts of kindness and help others without expecting anything in return.

- Make time for hobbies and activities that bring you joy and a sense of accomplishment.

5. Positive and Happier Life:
  - Prioritize self-care by maintaining a balanced diet, regular exercise, and sufficient sleep.
  - Nurture meaningful relationships and foster strong connections with loved ones.
  - Seek professional help, if necessary, to address mental health concerns or emotional issues.

By incorporating these elements into your daily life, you can create a Circle of Happiness that fosters a positive mindset, promotes healthier habits, and leads to a more satisfying and joyful life.

Let's look at seven examples of positive mind talk as outlined by Jay Shetty, British author, storyteller, and former monk:

1. When trying something new, doesn't go as planned. "I choose to put myself out there and although it's scary, I'm proud of myself for taking a chance. I'm growing with every new thing I try." Instead of beating yourself up over things you can't change, feel good and proud for having tried.

2. When apologizing for small things. "I don't need to apologize for every little thing. People are understanding and accepting of me, including myself. Over-apologizing is easy to do, and it's a form of self-deprecation. The next time a knee-jerk apology appears in your brain, switch it out for something more useful.

3. When facing fears head-on. "Even though I feel afraid, I don't shrink away from fear and because of that, I understand the strength of my inner power a little bit better." While parts of feeling afraid are normal and will always be there, gently approach your fear with love and understanding.

4. **When telling someone how you really** will always be better than staying silent. I say what I need to say, in the exact way I need to say it, and others need to hear it."

Instead of repeatedly replaying your moment of honesty in your head like a movie and critiquing every word, feel confident in your communication skills.

5. **When dealing with rejection.** "This wasn't the right door for me. I always try my best, but the outcome is not in my control. What's meant for me will not pass me. I choose to view everything, even this, as a blessing." No matter how much practice you get, rejection never feels good. Balance it out by twisting every situation into an opportunity for gratitude.

6. **When wanting to break a bad habit.** "I've been doing this for some time now. I understand it's not good for me. I choose forgiveness and deliberate change. Tomorrow is a new day to honor me with better decisions." Falling into bad habits can

happen like clockwork. Once you become aware of what's going on, it's up to you to forgive yourself and adjust accordingly.

7. **When feeling insecure.** "Feeling this way is understandable. But I am not seeing myself clearly. I am more capable than I realize. Every single day I am growing in self-love, self-confidence, and self-worth."

It's common for doubt and uncertainty to arise when we least expect them, leaving us unsure about ourselves without any apparent reason. In such moments, choosing to respond with self-love and compassion is crucial. Embracing a positive mindset requires consistent practice, particularly in the way we talk to ourselves.

By being intentional with our thoughts and choosing positive mind-talk every day, we can nourish our minds with kindness and build a more resilient, confident self. Our minds are delicate ecosystems that require continual nourishment with loving and kind thoughts. So, let's be mindful of the power of our minds and intentionally design our lives with positivity and self-belief.

As we embark on this journey together, taking proactive steps towards your personal growth is essential. To achieve this, actively engage in the following call-to-action activities. If you've been putting off adopting new habits, now is the perfect time to shift your mindset. Immerse yourself and participate wholeheartedly, without leaving any room for the excuse that you can do it later.

Call to Action

Activity 1

Purpose: Determine the essential steps you must undertake today or tomorrow to move forward and progress on your goals/dreams.

Instructions

1. Consider what you would like to accomplish today. Alternatively, create a list of things you aim to achieve tomorrow.
2. Take a moment to pause and reflect on your goals.
3. Make a list of actions you can take to move one step closer to your goals and dreams today.

Activity 2

Purpose: To engage in a self-dialogue

Instructions

1. Try speaking to yourself in the third person (e.g., Rahul is a positive person) if you are wavering between two decisions.

2. Initiate a conversation within yourself as you would speak to your friends. Communicate openly and honestly, fostering a nurturing internal environment.

3. Please prepare a comprehensive list of each decision's pros and cons and say them out loud.

Remember, engaging in self-dialogue is a valuable tool for personal and professional growth. Embrace this practice to unlock a deeper understanding of yourself and the world around you.

Activity 3
Purpose: Cultivate the habit of consistently working towards your goals.
Instructions

1. Each morning, as soon as you wake up (whether it's when you get out of bed, while showering, or during

your prayer and meditation time at home), think of one thing you'd like to achieve that day.

2. Consider how close accomplishing that task will bring you to your day's goals.
3. Once you have your answer, reflect on how much closer it will move you towards your long-term life goals.

Remember, success is built on consistent, intentional action. Keep working towards your goals, one step at a time, and you'll be well on your way to achieving your dreams.

As you become comfortable with accomplishing one task daily, gradually increase it to two and three. Be mindful not to overcommit yourself by attempting to complete more than three tasks in a day. The aim is to set you up for success. Throughout this journey, remember that we may encounter setbacks, but they're there to teach us how to rise stronger.

"If you fail, never give up because F.A.I.L. means *'First Attempt in Learning'*!" -Dr. A.P.J. Abdul Kalam

Chapter Takeaways

- The chapter emphasizes the importance of mind-talk and provides a suggested call to action for integrating it into your daily routine. A crucial factor that sets successful individuals apart from those who fail is positive mind-talk. Therefore, developing the habit of engaging in positive mind-talk can help reprogram your brain for happiness.

- When practicing mind-talk, using third-person pronouns, such as your name, is beneficial instead of "I." This technique creates a sense of distance between you and your thoughts, enabling you to be more objective and supportive.

- To unleash the full potential of your mind, it's important to develop a regular practice of engaging in activities that challenge your brain. These may include things like solving puzzles, playing games, or learning new skills, all of which can help improve cognitive function and keep your mind sharp and active. Please review 10 Golden Rules of Mental Mastery by Robin Sharma, they are a set of guidelines designed to help individuals develop a strong and resilient mindset. These rules include things like prioritizing self-care, focusing on growth and learning, and practicing gratitude and positivity.

- The Circle of Happiness is a comprehensive method for attaining a more satisfying, joyful, and well-balanced life. The elements include positive mind-talk, positive mindset, positive thoughts, and positive actions, eventually leading to a positive and happier life.

- As you cultivate the habit of mind-talk, remember to be gentle with yourself and avoid falling into the trap of negative self-talk.

I encourage you to share your success stories on the Habits4MIRACLES Facebook page to inspire others and reinforce the effectiveness of positive mind-talk.

"The best way to get a good idea is to have a lot of ideas." - Linus Paulding

CHAPTER 2

Igniting the Inner I *"Ideation"*

You had an impeccable idea. It excites you; you cannot wait to dig into it later. However, you could not recall the idea or anything pertaining to it after some time. That was aggravating, to say the least.

When was the last time that this happened to you? I think we can all agree that every single one of us has experienced this at least once. We have brilliant ideas right before falling asleep, only to forget them the next day. No matter what we do, we cannot recall them.

Ideation is a crucial tool for encouraging creativity and innovation. This chapter will explore techniques to get past the tendency to forget. But first, let us understand what ideation is really all about.

Have you ever heard the phrase there is "power in the pen?" Ideation is the creative process of originating, developing, and expressing new ideas. The stages of any thought process are involved from the inception of thought to its development and realization. Indeed, penning your ideas, even if they are still embryonic, offers you the "raw material" you can later develop.

To let you in on a personal anecdote, my mentor, Dr. Delatorro McNeal, asked his *Crush the Stage* event attendees to submit a list of the personal stories we would want to include in our speeches. We struggled to come up with no more than five stories, since we had not prepared any part of the list beforehand and had to think of ideas on the spot. To come up with such ideas quickly, we had to engage in a mind-mapping exercise for an hour. We wrote about our personal experiences that have benefited our lives and have the potential to inspire our audience during a speech. We began by categorizing our life experiences into three phases: our childhood, our college, or first job days, and the last five to seven years of our lives. In less than an hour, I listed eighteen life events that I felt shaped my life. Wow!

When I talk about this mind mapping exercise, please don't assume that you will do it the Sherlock way; that is not how it works in real life. Thoughts and ideas come to us in bursts of inspiration. It is almost nearly impossible for one to adequately conduct extensive brainstorming without forgetting some ideas that come to mind. The process that did wonders for me, once I employed them in my daily life, included:

- Practicing positive mind talk regularly.
- Journaling my thoughts, even those still in the embryonic stage.
- Developing these ideas by speaking with an expert or mentor.
- Acting on at least one of these ideas daily.

It is also important to note that these ideas come to you as you practice positive mind talk, and we must remember that a vision is nothing without action. As a result, we must pay close attention to our ideas as they arrive. The key is to jot them down as they come. The more you write them down or engage with them, the more they will keep flourishing. However, rather than filling a whiteboard with multiple ideas to be left unattended, and those not implemented, we must learn how to weed out the unnecessary.

As the chapter title suggests, we need to ignite our *Inner I* – ideation. To achieve this, we need to cleanse and declutter our minds. Ideation enables us to generate and nurture our unique ideas. Several paid or free apps can help you keep track of ideas. I use notes on my iPhone.

On average, a person can have forty-eight thoughts in a single minute. Wow! With that being the case, you might want to consider maintaining a journal if you've ever had trouble recalling a brilliant idea, a detailed memory, or a particular thought.

Writing in a journal is like sowing the seeds of ideas, the fruits of which you can reap later. Journaling is also therapeutic because it helps declutter mind fog and provides a means for healthy self-expression while coping with overwhelming emotions. Let's ponder on some benefits of journaling.

- Positively impact mental health by providing an outlet for emotional expression and reducing stress.
- Helps determine what makes you anxious or stressed when you have an issue. You can develop a strategy to address the problems and lessen your stress once you have identified your stressors.
- Helps you bring order to your life when everything seems chaotic. You learn more about yourself by sharing your thoughts, ideas, and emotions.

However, speaking from experience, I know how often we undervalue and disregard the benefits of releasing and journaling our thoughts. I did that, too. One reason behind that could be the lack of immediate and tangible results. Still, journaling helps our mental health in the long run. Consider your personal journaling time as valuable downtime where you can unwind and relax. Be assured that what you're doing is healthy for your body and mind.

Ideation is a process that one cannot achieve overnight. To make the ideation process a part of your daily life, consider implementing the following call-to-action activities.

Call to Action

Activity 1
Purpose: Cultivate positive mind-talk.
Instructions

1. To harness the power of positive thoughts and influence your outcomes, try implementing the following strategies:
   - Practice affirmations regularly, write them on sticky notes, and display them in visible locations
   - Take regular breaks to seek out and engage with uplifting content, such as quotes, articles, books, videos, and movies
   - Surround yourself with a supportive circle of friends who promote positivity and encourage personal growth.

2. Take some time to reflect on your relationships and evaluate the people you engage with on a regular basis

3. Evaluate the emotions and energy that emerge from your interactions with these people. Do they inspire positive feelings? If not, consider expanding your circle to include individuals who radiate positivity and support your journey towards a positive mindset.

Activity 2
Purpose: Journaling your thoughts
Instructions

1. Every day, set aside time to write. This makes it easier for you to keep up with journaling.

2. Keep a pen and paper nearby or use notes on your electronic devices. It will be easier to jot down your thoughts as they come to you. There is no set format that your journaling must adhere to. It is your own private space. Let your thoughts and words flow freely.

3. Get inspired and try to make the whole process fun!

Activity 3
Purpose: Identifying an ideal mentor
Instructions

Recognizing the significant impact that an expert or mentor can have on your personal and professional growth is essential. If you're having difficulty finding the right mentor, consider the following tips:

1. Explore professional networks such as LinkedIn to identify individuals who are actively sharing insights and expertise in your desired field of mentorship.
2. Instead of sending a pre-written generic request, send a personalized invitation that shows you have been paying attention to and learning from their contributions.

You might run into a mentor any place if you are open to new encounters and interactions. Strike up conversations with strangers and learn more about the people you already know. You might even find your mentor at your go-to restaurant or a coffee shop! If you are facing issues finding the right mentor and feel we have had a fruitful journey, you can always reach out to me.

Chapter Takeaways

- The subject of ideation, comprising methods for generating novel and innovative ideas in everyday life, was explored in this chapter. Journaling is a great way to keep track of your thoughts, produce, and record more creative ideas as they come to you.
- To integrate ideation into your routine, you can adopt a systematic approach, which includes practicing positive mind-talk, recording your thoughts and ideas in a journal, consulting with a mentor or an expert to refine your ideas, and committing to taking consistent action on at least one of your ideas.

- Journaling offers several advantages, such as enhancing mental well-being, identifying anxiety triggers, providing a sense of organization during chaotic times, and facilitating self-discovery.

Join Habits4miracles Facebook page and share your success stories to inspire and empower others to generate new ideas through effective ideation strategies. Let's create a community of ideation champions!

"Reading is a very necessary habit for every successful businessperson...It broadens your mind, helps with your written and verbal communication skills, and gives you a certain level of understanding and empathy." - Ellen Parry Lewis

CHAPTER 3

The Treasure Island of <u>R</u> *"Reading"*

There is a reason people state books are your best friends. Not only do they improve your mood and confidence, but they also help in reducing stress. Taking time out for yourself when you have a busy schedule can be more demanding than one might imagine.

Let's consider your typical day. If it solely comprises attending to your obligations at work or home, you may need to rethink your schedule. How do we get the time to do the things that can really help with personal development, especially when there is already so much on our plate? Well, you must start slowly and instill the habit of reading.

If you make reading books a habit, you will eventually become more drawn to books. Reading helps you unwind after a difficult day at work or school. Therefore, it is paramount to set aside time for reading, no matter how packed your schedule might be. And don't worry, there is never a wrong time to read.

If you're someone who dislikes reading, I want to encourage you to give it another try. Reading is a great way to embrace new perspectives and can be fun. Consider starting with a book in a genre that interests you or trying out an audiobook to make the experience more engaging. With time, you may discover a newfound love for reading and all the benefits it has to offer.

You do not need to be a voracious reader to inculcate the habit of reading. Growing up, even though I was never an avid reader, I managed to go to the library and spend a few hours there weekly. I developed this habit by watching my parents; both are still voracious readers today. I began reading self-development books in college, which was around the time when I first picked up the habit.

Since I have never been interested in reading fiction, I first decided which areas fascinated me the most: leadership, organizational behavior, learning, and self-development. Understanding various topics, case studies, and success stories is helpful as a public speaker and a learning professional. It has helped me immensely! Reading books has undoubtedly contributed to expanding my knowledge and boosting my confidence when engaging in conversations with friends, mentors, and teachers. As my confidence grew, I recognized the importance of incorporating this habit into my daily routine. I can attribute the implementation of the learnings acquired through my reading habit to the significant influence on my personality and the development of my overall facilitation and public speaking skills. This daily practice has greatly enhanced my ability to communicate effectively and confidently in various situations.

Dedicating five pages a day to reading may increase your knowledge by around one book per month. Researchers from Carnegie Mellon University found that the volume of white matter in the brain's language area improved throughout a six-month daily reading program. According to another research study, reading boosts cognitive performance, especially in older people.

In addition to reading for pleasure, many people read to broaden their knowledge or learn new skills. However, reading for work is also beneficial. It improves vocabulary, fosters creativity, lowers stress, and develops empathy. These elements are advantageous for professional life. So, there is some truth in the fact that a person is only one book away from fulfilling their desires or attaining their dreams.

A different study discovered that reading might increase a person's lifespan. More than 3,600 people were examined for this study for over twelve years, published in 2017 in *Innovation in Aging*.

Throughout the trial, those who read books had a reduced risk of dying and lived longer on average than those who read nothing or only read magazines and newspapers.

As an employer or business owner, if you are wondering how reading can affect a workplace and its employees, let me share this nugget. Reading is a valuable and effective way to become knowledgeable and well-versed in a particular topic. By reading widely and consistently, we can expand our understanding and expertise in a subject matter.

Reading about various topics makes one more likely to be well-rounded. Both are qualities that business owners should look for in their employees and themselves.

Please allow me to share some lesser-known benefits of reading:

1. **Improved sleep:** Studies have shown that reading a book before going to bed can improve both the quality and quantity of sleep.

2. **Empathy development:** Reading fictional books can increase empathy by helping readers understand and relate to characters' emotions and experiences.

3. **Memory improvement:** Reading can enhance memory and cognitive function, especially in older adults.

4. **Social connectedness:** Reading can help people feel more connected to others by providing a common topic of discussion and facilitating conversations.

5. **Brain stimulation:** Reading can stimulate the brain's neural pathways, keeping the mind active and reducing the risk of cognitive decline.

I hope that I have motivated you to consider incorporating reading into your daily routine. Let's explore some actionable steps that can help you make reading a habit, allowing you to apply the lessons learned from books and eBooks to design your life your way.

Call to Action

Activity 1
Purpose: Set a reading goal
Instructions

1. Schedule a daily reading time for at least 5 to 10 minutes, even if that requires getting up 30 minutes earlier than usual.

2. Make plans to read during lunch or dinner breaks or early hours before leaving for work.

3. Put your reading habits on your priority list by turning them into precise, deadline-driven goals.

4. Move to 20 minutes daily. Use a simple timer to track your progress. Even though it may appear insignificant at first, it quickly adds up,

and your reading capacity will improve over time.

Bonus Tip - Consider using your local library's free listening app in addition to audible.

Activity 2
Purpose: Create a T.B.R. (To Be Read) list.
Instructions

1. Research curated book lists from leaders you respect or in your field of interest to save time while choosing books. These lists often contain highly recommended and impactful books.
2. Reach out to people you admire or successful individuals in your field for their favorite book recommendations. This could provide you with unique and valuable insights.
3. Consult with friends and colleagues about their recent reads or favorite books. Their suggestions might introduce you to new authors or genres

you haven't explored yet.

4. Visit a bookstore or browse online bookstores to discover exciting titles for your reading list. Don't forget to check out bestseller lists and staff recommendations, as they often feature high-quality books.

5. When building your TBR list, consider vetting books by reading summaries before committing to them. Services like <u>Blinkist</u> offer concise summaries of many popular books, helping you make informed decisions.

Activity 3
Purpose: Instill reading as a habit
Instructions

By integrating these below strategies, you can increase your motivation to read consistently and make it an integral part of your daily life, enhancing your overall personal and intellectual growth.

1. **Keep reading materials handy:** Always carry some reading material with you, be it a physical book, an eBook on your smartphone, or an eBook reader. This way, you can seize any opportunity to read during unexpected downtime.

2. **Join a book club or reading group:** Connect with like-minded individuals who share your interests and are passionate readers. This will provide accountability and promote engaging discussions, enhancing your understanding of the materials.

3. **Swap entertainment forms:** Make a conscious effort to replace other forms of entertainment with reading. For instance, choose to read a book instead of watching TV, playing video games, or browsing social media platforms like Instagram or Facebook.

4. **Keep reading enjoyable:** Reading should be a pleasurable activity. If you find that you're not enjoying a book, don't be afraid to move on and try something else. Finding books that genuinely interest and captivate you is essential, making reading a rewarding experience.

Chapter Takeaways

• This chapter emphasizes the significance of cultivating a reading habit for personal growth and provides practical tips to establish a consistent reading routine. Reading expands knowledge, empathy, and imagination, and can serve as a stress-reliever after a hectic day.

• Even if you do not enjoy reading, it is worth giving it another chance to discover new perspectives and find enjoyment in it. Additionally, reading promotes critical thinking skills and can improve brain structure. Encouraging reading habits in the workplace can strengthen relationships among colleagues.

• Begin by allocating at least 20 minutes daily for reading, which may appear insignificant initially but can yield significant long-term benefits.

• The action plans outlined in the chapter may serve as an excellent foundation for incorporating reading habits into your everyday life. Initiating practices such as developing a To Be Read (TBR) list, examining book summaries before purchase, participating in a book club, or engaging with a community of book enthusiasts on social media, and replacing other forms of entertainment with reading could make a significant impact.

Join the Habits4Miracles Facebook page and share your personal experiences on how reading has favorably impacted your personal development, or request assistance in embracing reading as a habit. Your input can inspire others to explore creative ways to integrate reading into their daily routines.

"The ultimate authority must always rest with the individual's own reason and critical analysis." - Dalai Lama

CHAPTER 4

The Easy **A** *"Analyzation"*

Let's ponder what Nelson Mandela once said: "I never lose – I either win or learn." Self-Analysis is taking the time to reflect on and learn from our actions. Adopting this strategy can be comforting, since you can find solace because you won't truly make mistakes if you change your perspective.

Analyzing outcomes is a vital aspect of the ideation and execution process. It is essential to remember that this analysis is not solely focused on breaking down complex data sets but also involves self-reflection. Some benefits of self-analysis include:

1. **Gaining new perspectives:** By evaluating your actions and decisions, you can get a different perspective, identify improvement areas, and generate new ideas to pursue.

2. **Confidence in your abilities:** Reflecting on your successes and learning experiences can boost your self-confidence and help you feel more capable of tackling challenges.

3. **Curious Learner:** Analyzing your performance can ignite a desire to find creative solutions to problems and inspire you to learn new skills.

4. **Increased accountability:** Self-analysis allows you to take responsibility for your actions, understand the consequences of your choices, and make better decisions in the future.

By engaging in self-analysis, you can enhance your personal and professional growth, ultimately improving your overall effectiveness in bringing your ideas to fruition.

Let me share one of my personal stories regarding how I employed the analysis method earlier. One crucial decision I had to make during my Masters in Business Administration (MBA) program was to choose a specialization (aka major). In essence, at the beginning of the third semester, we were required to select a specialization. Around the time of pursuing my M.B.A., finance was the second-most popular choice, followed by marketing. For some reason, I didn't feel fulfilled enough to pursue a career in either of these disciplines.

I discovered that because I enjoy reading self-help books, I have a strong desire to assist others in realizing their dreams. As a result, my choices were more inclined toward human resource management and operations management. I consulted with my professors, some alumni, and friends; they all suggested that I do an internship to see if human resources would best suit me and my future. I also connected with a few H.R. professionals to better comprehend their daily lives.

We had to complete an internship in the summer as part of our coursework. As I knew it would be too late, nearing the end of the first semester, I considered using my Christmas break to complete my internship. Thanks to my brother-in-law, I landed a one-month internship at *Tetra Pak.*

In addition to finishing my winter project, I had the chance to assist Tetra Pak's H.R. team and learn more about the department's day-to-day functions. With time, I realized that one must manage many aspects of H.R. besides employee development.

I am grateful to the Head of H.R. at Tetra Pak for giving me a chance to help their team; it was also through his recommendation that I was able to land my next internship in the summer at Pepsi's H.R. division.

One of my fondest work experiences was at Pepsi, where I had the chance to collaborate with leaders from many departments and support the H.R. team's daily operations. My greatest gratification came from watching employees' faces light up when I resolved their queries. And upon completion of the two internships, I pursued my specialization in Human Resources.

I hope my little anecdote gives you an idea of how one can employ the habit of analyzing in your daily life. To sum it all up for you, I took the following course of action during the analytical process:

- Identified the end goal.
- Researched and consulted with mentors or people who could offer advice.
- Decided on the next steps and took action.

While analysis is essential in decision-making and problem-solving, it's crucial to avoid over-analyzing or analysis paralysis. Over-analyzing a situation can lead to indecisiveness, inaction, and missed opportunities. It can also lead to burnout and exhaustion, as the constant scrutiny and examination can be mentally and emotionally draining. Instead, it's important to strike a balance between analysis and action. Gathering relevant information and considering different perspectives is vital, but setting a deadline for making a decision or taking action is equally important. By doing so, we can avoid getting stuck in the analysis phase and ensure that we make progress towards achieving our goals.

To get meaningful and measurable results in the right direction, we must avoid overthinking, commit to action, and avoid being reactive. Doing this will require specific judgments and action plans to address complex issues more easily. I think discussing Steven Covey's ideas of the "circle of concern" and "circle of influence" from his book, *7 Habits of Highly Effective*

People, would help you understand a bit more.

A circle of concern encompasses aspects of life or business that are beyond our control. These may include global events, the economy, or other people's decisions and actions. On the other hand, a circle of influence represents areas where we have the power to make a difference, such as our own behaviors, choices, and attitudes.

Focusing on the circle of concern can lead to feelings of frustration and helplessness, as we are unable to control or change these external factors. In contrast, directing our attention towards our circle of influence allows us to take proactive measures and make a tangible impact on our personal and professional lives.

By concentrating on areas where we have control, we can effectively utilize our time and energy to create positive change. This approach fosters personal growth and development and enhances our ability to adapt to and influence external circumstances. It is crucial to recognize the distinction between our circle of concern and circle of influence. By shifting our focus from concerns to areas where we can make a difference, we can achieve greater success, satisfaction, and overall well-being.

According to Covey, one way to determine which circle our concern is in is to distinguish between the have's and the be's. The circle of concern is filled with the have's – "if I had a degree" or "if I had a better boss;" whereas circle of influence is filled with the be's - I can be more patient, be wise, be loving. It's the character focus.

Most of the time, we focus on changing our lives and don't take the time to reflect on our prior conduct or actions. Thus, we need to take a moment to reflect on actions or behaviors that have worked well for us. Instead of concentrating too much on where we need to improve, we must play to our strengths.

As a learning professional, I have seen an increase in the number of people who can't seem to "get out of their own way." They don't make good choices and are aware of this. Even if they want to make a better choice and intend to make a different decision in the future, they still don't. They continue to dwell on cyclic routines and old narratives.

Over the years, I have become more conscious of how much my daily decisions and choices are affected by my narratives or how I see myself. I have also realized how often our decision-making is influenced by self-esteem and mind talk. You know that small voice inside drives most of our actions and thoughts without permission.

I agree that everyone has their own motivations and reasons for their actions, often driven by their unique experiences and perspectives. To embark on a journey of self-improvement without feeling overwhelmed, consider implementing these simple call-to-action steps.

Call to Action

Activity 1

Purpose: Steps to instill the habit of self-analysis
Instructions

1. Observe your daily routines, habits, and actions. Ask yourself why you do certain things and how they contribute to your overall well-being and goals.
2. Seek feedback from trusted friends, family, or mentors. They can provide valuable insights into your strengths and weaknesses.
3. Practice daily reflection on your thoughts, emotions, and behaviors without judgment.
4. Set achievable goals for self-improvement based on your analysis. Focus on small steps that you can take daily to achieve them.
5. Continuously monitor your progress and adjust your actions accordingly.

Celebrate your successes while learning from your failures.

Activity 2
Purpose: Overcoming "Analysis Paralysis"
Instructions

1. Recognize when you are constantly overthinking a situation or decision.
2. Take a step back and evaluate your current emotions. Are you feeling overwhelmed, anxious, or stressed? Acknowledge these feelings and try to identify their source.
3. Engage in a hobby or activity that you enjoy. Activities can help distract you from overthinking and give you a fresh perspective. Try something new, such as cooking, painting, drawing, dancing, or hiking.
4. Establish a deadline for making a decision or taking action. Giving yourself a specific timeline can help you avoid getting stuck in indecision and move forward with confidence.

Activity 3
Purpose: Know yourself
Instructions

1. I recommend taking a free online "know yourself" assessment such as.

   - **16Personalities:** This website offers a free personality test based on the Myers-Briggs Type Indicator (MBTI).

   - **VIA Institute on Character:** This website offers a free character strengths assessment to help you identify your core strengths and virtues.

   - **Truity:** This website offers a variety of free personality tests, including the Big Five personality traits and the Enneagram.

   - **CareerOneStop:** This website, sponsored by the U.S. Department of Labor, offers free career assessments to help you identify your interests, skills, and values.

- **Open Psychometrics:** This website offers a collection of free personality tests and quizzes, including tests for emotional intelligence, personality disorders, and more.

These assessments will reveal how much you know about yourself. When we clearly understand who we are, what we value, and want, we are better equipped to make decisions and pursue our goals. Without a strong sense of self, we may feel lost, unsure of our direction or purpose.

2. After taking these assessment tests, reflect on the results to identify your strengths and areas of improvement.

3. Seek feedback from trusted sources, such as friends, family, or a mentor. They may provide insights and perspectives that you may have overlooked.

Chapter Takeaways

- Examining your mind talk is one of the most important steps toward personal growth. Analyzing is slowing down to evaluate and draw lessons from our past actions. Self-analysis can be a powerful tool for personal growth and development, helping us to identify our strengths, overcome our weaknesses, and achieve our goals.

- Understanding ourselves more deeply offers advantages such as acquiring new viewpoints, building confidence in our skills, fostering curiosity for learning, and enhancing personal accountability.

- Overthinking or overanalyzing a problem can hinder decision-making and prevent us from achieving our goals within a reasonable time frame. It is important to strike a balance between analysis and action to avoid getting stuck in analysis paralysis. By engaging in hobbies, setting deadlines, and seeking support, we can maintain focus on our goals and achieve greater success.

- Concentrate on things that are within your control or influence, rather than those outside of your control.

- Remember that self-analysis is a continuous process requiring patience, dedication, and self-awareness. Keep in mind that the ultimate goal is to understand yourself better and make positive changes that will enhance your personal and professional life.

Join Habits4Miracles Facebook group to connect with like-minded individuals who share a passion for personal growth. Together, we can inspire and support each other on this transformative journey of self-discovery. Don't miss this opportunity to thrive – come, be a part of our empowering community!

"To increase speed, you must increase the amount of rest, peace, and calmness that you can maintain. That is the secret to playing fast." - Pepe Romero

CHAPTER 5

The Winding Path to C *"Calmness"*

Eventhough it may seem inevitable, panicking seldom solves anything. In the moment, we gravitate to its hold; however, even though the panic has occurred, nothing has improved or gotten slightly better.

A helpful technique I often employ is reminding myself of past experiences in similar situations. When faced with a complex circumstance, I reflect on how I managed a comparable situation before and persevered through it. This helps me avoid panicking during challenging situations.

You take a moment to declare to yourself, "You've got this [insert your name]!" In case this sounds familiar, we discussed this in the first chapter of this book on mind-talk, and it is one of the most effective ways to help keep calm. How can you achieve that?

During my formative years, my father encouraged me to join a cricket academy for children under eighteen. The rigorous three-hour daily regimen, including weekend games, was intense, but I was determined to improve. As I progressed, I discovered that I performed well against slow bowlers (spinners) but struggled when facing fast bowlers. Despite my efforts to train and prepare myself, the stress and pressure made it difficult to perform well.

During a one-on-one session with my coach, I realized I was overthinking the game's outcome and not focusing on the joy of playing. I was worried about not contributing enough to the team, which affected my performance. It took time, but I learned to maintain my composure, avoid obsessing over the result, and reject unnecessary stress.

My coach's guidance helped me feel more confident in my abilities, and I could remain composed and focused during the next game. Instead of worrying about the outcome, I concentrated on keeping my eyes on the ball and enjoying the game. This shift in the mindset of enjoying the moment was a game-changer, and I could contribute to helping my team win.

This experience taught me that a clear and focused mind is crucial to performing at our best. When we let go of unnecessary stress and focus on the joy of the task at hand, we can operate at our full potential.

Being calm is a state or virtue of not being agitated, excited, or disturbed. In this sense, calmness is a state of mind rather than an emotion. Particular techniques or activities, such as meditation, may regulate it. When we are calm, we can make better decisions.

While everybody gets irritated and feels anger as a normal emotion, learning how to channel that anger is crucial. It is still a work in progress for me and many others, and that is okay!

It is also important to note that no feeling is wrong or right, but how we display our anger matters. We must communicate our anger in a controlled and constructive way, as it might impact the other individual more than we can imagine. Why should we aspire to reach a state of calm?

The advantages are our ability to control our thoughts, feelings, and actions. Being calm also enables us to concentrate our attention on the problem and not on the rage that is rooted in the situation. Once you become upset, it is much more challenging to regain your composure. That is, unfortunately, a well-known fact. Seldom can people keep calm 100% of the time. If you find it difficult to stay composed, I introduce you to a method that Ellen Mishel calls "faking calm."

Here is how you can implement it in your daily life:

- Breathe slowly and consciously. While you do so, keep counting down from ten to one or zero. You can also try breathing from your belly. Place your left hand on your stomach and take a deep breath. Exhale through your mouth while pushing your stomach to release the air.
- Say to yourself, "It is okay to feel this way, and I can handle this."
- Close your eyes and visualize yourself relaxing far away on a tropical island, strolling through a meadow, or visiting your dream destination.
- Avoid stiffening the eye muscles or agitated, anxious, or angry. Maintain a neutral expression on your face if you cannot cope with the stressful scenario.
- If you find you are having trouble communicating, take time for a few minutes and let the other person know. Taking time out will help you collect your thoughts before discussing things with the other person.

I have also noticed that calm leaders or managers foster more trust in workplaces and are more efficient. Not only do the employees feel more drawn to creating healthy relationships with them, but they also look up to them. Leaders or managers who are calm and collected, instead of impetuous, anxious, or prone to fury, are more likely to inspire people and build trust in the workplace. These Leaders or managers also breed healthy loyalty.

Why is being calm so important, and does the lack of it mean you are not a good leader or a manager? Certainly not. You can be a great manager, but your management style also sets the tone for your team's perception of your ability to lead. It also impacts the outcomes you will produce collectively. If you have a calm-assertive personality type, you can convey objectives while being calm, collected, and level-headed. You also plan things better and know the most efficient way to get things done.

So, here are a few strategies that can help you be that leader or manager of everyone's dreams:

- Be consistent with your expectations. Ensure that your expectations are congruent with the expectations of the team. Consider a situation where employees often fail to submit their weekly reports, despite your explicit expectations. In this situation, you can *calmly* exert your authority because it is based on mutually accepted principles.

- Consider your options carefully before making a choice or taking a step. If an employee fails to meet your standards or breaches business policy, thoroughly weigh your decisions before acting. Be very patient and methodical in your approach.

- Communicate with your team members clearly and firmly. Being assertive means speaking with your team honestly and openly while being confident in your management style and what you offer. Poised managers can be direct and pragmatic without being critical or insensitive.

Let's review some actionable steps we can take to bring more calmness into our daily routine.

Call to Action

Activity 1

Purpose: Take a periodic break from your schedule and make a conscious effort to cultivate a calm and centered mindset.

Instructions

If you're experiencing anxiety or agitation, consider trying the following relaxation techniques:

- Take a moment to pause and put away any electronic devices, ensuring they are on silent mode.
- Close your eyes and allow your breath to flow naturally.
- Try taking deep breaths in through your nose and out through your mouth.
- Inhale slowly and steadily, counting from one to five. This can be helpful for some individuals.

- Practice this for at least five minutes, maintaining a steady and consistent breathing pattern.

Activity 2
Purpose: Strategies to help you remain calm the next time you encounter a situation that feels out of control.
Instructions

1. The first thing to do when something unexpected happens and throws you off is to distance yourself from the scenario rather than react immediately.

2. Another technique to gain perspective on the situation is to do something that takes you out of your current frame of mind. To achieve this, the five-step 54321 grounding exercise is a favorite of many therapists and will help you (and your kids) during periods of stress, anxiety, or even when you need a little break.

5-4-3-2-1 Technique

Using the 5-4-3-2-1 technique, you will purposefully take in the details of your surroundings using each of your senses. Strive to notice small details that your mind would usually tune out, such as distant sounds, or the texture of an ordinary object.

What are 5 things you can see? Look for small details such as a pattern on the ceiling, the way light reflects off a surface, or an object you never noticed.

What are 4 things you can feel? Notice the sensation of clothing on your body, the sun on your skin, or the feeling of the chair you are sitting in. Pick up an object and examine its weight, texture, and other physical qualities.

What are 3 things you can hear? Pay special attention to the sounds your mind has tuned out, such as a ticking clock, distant traffic, or trees blowing in the wind.

What are 2 things you can smell? Try to notice smells in the air around you, like an air freshener or freshly mowed grass. You may also look around for something that has a scent, such as a flower or an unlit candle.

What is 1 thing you can taste? Carry gum, candy, or small snacks for this step. Pop one in your mouth and focus your attention closely on the flavors.

Activity 3

Purpose: Cultivating a Habit of Calmness

Instructions

1. Incorporate calming activities into your daily routine to help you achieve your desired peace and tranquility. Consider activities such as meditation, reading, eating foods you enjoy, or listening to relaxing music or podcasts.

2. Engage in stress-relieving activities that involve using your hands, such as pottery or drawing. These activities can help distract your thoughts and promote calmness.

3. Add a brisk walk to your daily routine. Exercise releases endorphins, which can enhance mood, focus, and sleep.

Chapter Takeaways

- By learning to quiet the mind, you can build inner strength and become less and less dependent on external factors. Even though everyone feels annoyed, and anger is a common emotion, it is essential to learn how to control it. Strategies such as "Faking Calm" or 54321 Grounding technique can channel your feelings better.

- When you develop the skill of remaining composed under pressure, your concentration and creativity can be enhanced. Building your day around relaxing activities can help you stay calm and focused throughout the day.

- Maintaining a calm demeanor can positively affect how you perceive situations in life. Affirmations and positive thinking techniques are often utilized in developing calmness, leading to a more positive outlook on life.

- In a workplace, to excel as a preferred leader or manager, concentrate on: Upholding consistent expectations, carefully evaluating options before making choices, and communicating effectively with team members while demonstrating confidence in your management approach.

I encourage all our readers to embrace the power of calmness in their daily lives. For those who have already experienced the positive impact of practicing calmness, I invite you to share your success stories on the Habits4Miracles Facebook page. Your experiences can inspire others to adopt this valuable practice, fostering a supportive community where we can all grow together. Take the first step toward a more tranquil life and inspire others to do the same – join us in celebrating the power of calmness!

"At the center of your being, you have the answer; you know who you are, and you know what you want." - Lao Tzu

CHAPTER 6

The Law of L – *Listening*

When we consider the value of listening, we frequently relate it to the art of listening to what others say because it is essential for effective communication and dispute resolution. There is, however, another aspect to this: the crucial habit of listening to ourselves.

We can all agree that we each have remarkable gut instincts, which others often call the inner voice. We do not, however, often consider that we are our best consultants.

How do we change that? Something that I advise is to give yourself time to think before deciding, then proceed as needed. After all, it is with ourselves that we spend the most time on earth. So, let's pause momentarily and listen to ourselves and understand.

While I feel that we all understand, at varying levels, the value of listening, it is the nudge that helps us register the benefits. During one of my online coaching training sessions, I began looking for answers to the "power of hearing one's own story."

In one such session, our facilitator guided us through a group activity where we were instructed to turn off our microphones and the cameras. The facilitator explained it was because we needed to listen to ourselves talk and process whatever we said. As you can tell, my immediate thought was that it was weird.

Even though I was used to talking to myself, it felt awkward doing so with our cameras turned on, let alone doing it in front of everyone. The facilitator was not an active participant in our conversations with ourselves. Still, he started posing questions to help us navigate through the exercise. For the next few minutes, we spoke to our screens. That facilitator murmured, "Hmmm, hmmm…" while grinning and nodding as if he could hear all of us.

I often go back to that session, and even though it was atypical, it struck a chord and left a lasting impression. After we had unmuted ourselves, we discussed it with the group and the facilitator. Everyone expressed how significant and illuminating the conversation had been for us all. Oddly enough, while the situation may have seemed absurd to an outsider, it was a very moving experience that led to amazing realizations.

The point of my story was that listening to yourself – or "listening within," as some call it – entails becoming aware of your feelings, thoughts, and needs. While it could seem simple and something we all do, the reality is far from it.

It is challenging to listen to oneself in the world we live in today, especially being surrounded by factors that lure and distract us. This includes gadgets made to alert us at their convenience rather than ours. Listening to yourself is not some gimmick that may or may not work. It is very efficient and can lead you to a state where you understand yourself more, thereby ensuring your success.

On another note, we all know what emotional outbursts can do to us (and others!). They can catch you off guard and cause issues at work or in personal relationships if ignored for too long. This equates to the "elephant in the room." That saying means someone, or something, is being left unaddressed while taking up time and space.

According to a Canadian study by Alexa M Tullett and Michael Inzlicht, impulsive behavior is more prevalent among people who do not listen to their inner voice. You may often be mired in a cycle of negative thoughts without realizing it. And it is through positive mind talk and the habit of listening to yourself that you can come out of it.

I have also found that while most people do not know how to express their values, they are aware of them. This makes perfect sense because how else would we know what to do to be happy or content unless we listen to ourselves? Making decisions turns into a game of tic-tac-toe when you lack a reliable means of identifying your current needs, goals, and ideals. Thus, to prosper and find fulfillment, one must be consciously aware of their values and learn to listen to self. This is a step in the right direction towards personal development and, consequently, a more fulfilled life.

Dr. Julia Harper, occupational therapist and life coach, emphasizes listening to oneself and what you say. She also emphasizes the importance of understanding that talking to self involves speaking and listening, described as "self-awareness" and "self-listening."

The journey to self-awareness matters more than the destination. What you required yesterday might not be what you need right now to feel motivated, at ease, and clear-headed. Trusting yourself and taking care of yourself demands listening to your internal narrative. Because of your surroundings, experiences, and the people in your inner circle, your values may change throughout life. In such cases, you cannot be sure of the path you have undertaken if you do not listen to yourself. But making better decisions comes from being able to listen to yourself.

Your chances of comprehending your ideas and actions get significantly higher. What prevents you from listening to yourself?

- **The environment where you have grown up:** One aspect that often prevents people from listening to their inner voice is the environment in which they grew up. It can be challenging for those whose families did not encourage them to be who they are and have their own opinions or likes and dislikes. As a result, listening to oneself is often not given importance.

- **External pressures and their expectations:** We are constantly surrounded by people whose opinions are louder than ours. This often deafens the inner voice within us. Not only that, almost every decision we make is governed by what is expected of us and accepted by people.

- **Lack of life-work balance:** An imbalanced life-work schedule will affect your connection with yourself and your relationships with others. You might be unable to give yourself the time you need if you are constantly working or under a lot of unhealthy stress.

- **Excessive Screen time**: We can no longer avoid our screens because everything is now housed digitally. It would be naïve to claim that our screen time has not increased significantly over the past two years. As a result, because of the increase in screen time and the resulting overstimulation we experience, we frequently miss out on simply sitting with our thoughts and enjoying our own company.

No matter the stage you are at in your life right now, if you feel your inner voice has somewhat been buried, here are some actions that can help if employed regularly.

Call to Action

Activity 1

Purpose: To help reduce external distractions and improve listening skills.

Instructions

1. Take a moment to pause and set aside all electronic devices. Find a comfortable place to sit or stand.

2. Ask yourself meaningful questions and allow your thoughts to flow naturally. Consider questions related to your current situation, goals, and values. Write down your thoughts and reflections in a journal.

3. If you struggle to make a decision, try speaking to yourself in the third person. This can provide a helpful distance and allow for a fresh perspective.

4. Speak out loud or converse with yourself as if speaking to a friend or

trusted advisor. This can help you gain clarity and better understand your thoughts and feelings.

Activity 2
Purpose: Instilling the habit of self-listening
Instructions

1. Maintain a journal, a notes app on your phone, or another journaling platform (e.g., Penzu - complimentary for the basic version), which allows you to express your thoughts without fear of judgment or offending others. Writing ideas down naturally slows down your thought process, making it easier to listen to yourself clearly and eliminate distractions.

2. Commit to a daily self-check-in to assess your emotions and identify your values. Allocate dedicated time in your routine for introspection and self-discovery.

3. Engage in activities such as walking or swimming, which not only foster emotional well-being but also provide the

physical benefits of exercise. These activities help clear mental fog, enabling you to focus on self-reflection and inner exploration.

4. Invest time in reading, particularly personal development literature, and practice recommended exercises. Periodically pause to contemplate how to integrate these insights and habits into your daily life.

Activity 3
Purpose: Strategies for Practicing Self-Listening
Instructions

1. Engage in individual exercises and sports such as running on a circular track, repeatedly hitting a tennis ball against a wall, or swimming multiple laps. These activities, like walking, allow subconscious observations about yourself and your interactions with the world to emerge naturally.

2. Establishing clear boundaries is essential in various aspects of our lives, particularly when trying to attune to our inner voice. Prioritizing the opinions, demands, and needs of others over your own can suppress your inner voice. Cultivate self-trust, pause to reflect before committing to anything, and learn to assertively say no when necessary.

Chapter Takeaways

- Your inner voice can serve as a reliable guide, whether explicit or faint. Listening to your inner self can lead to the development of wisdom, whether providing guidance for the present, reflecting on the past, or pointing towards a particular path.
- Writing in a journal and going for a walk can assist in clearing mental fog. It is crucial to remember that these simple practices are often undervalued, and instead, we waste time talking on our phones or mindlessly scrolling through them.

- Engaging in activities such as taking "ME" time and reading can allow you to reflect on yourself. It is essential to select activities that are easy and convenient for you to do.

- To initiate a change, it's crucial to be attentive to your inner signals. Just recognizing them is not enough; taking action is of utmost importance. Once you have determined your needs and desires, the best move is to proceed in that direction.

- Certain factors can hinder our ability to listen to ourselves, including the environment in which we were raised, external pressures and expectations, a lack of balance between work and life, and excessive screen time.

Spread the power of self-listening by sharing it with your loved ones and joining the Habits4Miracles Facebook community. Help ignite the spark and propagate the hope of becoming the best version of oneself. Join us in promoting self-awareness and growth, inspiring others to embark on their personal development journey.

"To keep the body in good health is a duty…otherwise, we shall not be able to keep our mind strong and clear." - Buddha

CHAPTER 7

The Fruit of <u>E</u> *"Exercise"*

Are you often engulfed with overwhelming tiredness that isn't relieved by rest or sleep? Does leaving your bed every morning seem dreadful? No matter how many shots of coffee you consume? Do you find yourself slogging throughout the day with extraordinarily little energy? Well, you are not alone.

Two years after the pandemic, our bodies have not yet completely escaped survival mode because of the lack of time to process the trauma and fully heal. Post-pandemic fatigue seems to be the new normal because of prolonged stress and anxiety of unforeseen circumstances. Despite some people returning to their in-person workplaces, many individuals still work from home or use a hybrid model. No matter your work mode, maintaining a balance between work and life can be a real struggle.

Also, the pandemic has been an eye-opener, revealing the importance of self-care and its direct impact on our mental health. What is alarming is the neglect and stigma associated with mental health issues, which are as common as depression and anxiety, which have come to the forefront.

Let us go back and address the issues that we began with in the first place. How do we kick-start our day with positivity? How do we bring about the burst of energy and sustain it throughout the day?

One simple trick is to dedicate time to your daily routine for exercise. And by exercise, I do not mean signing up for a marathon or cranking out bench presses in the gym. It could be as simple as stretching, jumping jacks, or even taking a brisk walk for ten to fifteen minutes daily.

Do you need to change your entire schedule to incorporate a few minutes of exercising during the day? Or am I asking you to set unrealistic goals that disrupt your life? Start simple and slow. Always remember that less is more and that getting something is better than nothing regarding exercise. Growing by a mere 2% is better than doing nothing times 200%. As with any exercise or diet changes, consult your physician about your health and regimen.

If you are a foodie like I am and face challenges in controlling your portion size, working out for 10-15 minutes daily will be a blessing. I feel energized, charged, and happy on the days I swim. It's a different feeling altogether and is difficult to express. It lets me enjoy my favorite dishes without guilt.

To start, aim for a 10–15-minute workout session as your goal. Find it challenging to commit to this routine. This chapter will help you change your mindset and motivate you to exercise daily. But if you are one of those who has already formed an exercise routine, congratulations! You have won half the battle of incorporating self-care into your daily lifestyle.

Talking about self-care, shall we take a moment to reflect upon research that has found a direct link between self-care and our mental health? Physical activity releases feel-good endorphins, natural cannabis, e.g., brain chemicals that enhance your well-being.

Exercising makes you feel more energetic throughout the day, helping you sleep better at night and relax. This gives you a positive outlook toward life and boosts your self-confidence. It also acts as a powerful medicine for common mental health challenges. Trust me, nobody who has exercised has ever regretted it. It is time we stop aimlessly scrolling on social media and form a habit that our future selves will thank us for.

Let us once again look in brief at the benefits of implementing exercise consistently:

- **Improves mental health:** Research shows a clear association between fitness and mental health. Exercise is proven to reduce anxiety and treat long-term depression.
- **Reduces stress:** Exercise is known to help relax our muscles and relieve tension in the body. Cardiovascular exercise delivers oxygen and nutrients to your tissues, helps your cardiovascular system work more efficiently, and gives you more energy for your daily activities.
- **Makes you feel better:** Exercise helps stimulate those feel-good brain chemicals that lift your mood and relax you by reducing stress.
- **Boosts your confidence:** Exercise burns calories, prevents excess weight gain, and

ramps metabolism. It helps you maintain a positive body image.

- **Gives you a sharper memory:** Exercising every day tires you out and helps you fall asleep faster and sleep better at night. This, in turn, gives you a sharper memory and an increased ability to retain information.

In short, our body and mind are so closely linked that when our body feels better, so will our mind.

Now, in case our discussion was not enough motivation to get you started with your exercising journey, let us look at the journey of Vineeta Singh, C.E.O., and co-founder of SUGAR Cosmetics. "Whenever there is a stressful situation, I like to go for a run. You could say I am a running junkie," she says. Despite facing the worst phase of the pandemic and dealing with losses and businesses falling apart, as an entrepreneur, she never forgot to prioritize her health and fitness by putting on her running shoes.

She found running to be meditative and states, "It does have that breath work, you know, and you are one with yourself, and you get that clear, peaceful time. When your entire schedule gets disrupted, and there is a lot of stress, running is the one thing that happens at the same time every day – and it grounds me."

Let's turn to the 52-year-old country music star Tim McGraw, who says exercise is all about "feeling good and being where I want to be physically and on stage." In 2008, Tim McGraw introduced a massive change in his life by quitting alcohol, ditching fast food, and hitting the gym when his daughter expressed concern for his health. He was getting out of shape during the prime of his career. As *Men's Health* documents, McGraw also started his fitness journey with small steps. He incorporated light walks in the morning and eventually kept pushing the bar. Brisk morning walks soon turned into 20-minute runs and, ultimately, weightlifting.

"It wasn't like I was trying to lose 40 pounds; I just wanted to get healthy," says McGraw. He now creates a fun workout routine that pushes his physical limits simultaneously. This keeps him at the top of his game. McGraw is very proud of his transformation and advises people to take charge of things like their bodies that can be easily controlled before it is too late. Nothing is worse than knowing you need to exercise but waiting until you cannot do so.

Matt McGorry, an American actor, and activist rightly says, "The mind is the most important part of achieving any fitness goal. Mental change always comes before physical change." Here are some tips that can help you overcome the struggle of maintaining a consistent exercise routine.

1. **Change your perspective:** Exercising should be a conscious choice to care for your body and mind. Rather than thinking about it as a task, think about all the

benefits it will reap, and you will be more likely to engage/want to jump into an exercise routine.

2. **Bring in commitment:** Sticking to your routine is crucial to reap the maximum benefits of physical activity. Make it a point to adhere to the goals that you have set for yourself daily. Remember, there is no perfect day to start something. Make it happen, now!

3. **Make workout fun:** Adding variety to your workout routine will keep you coming back for more. Do exercises that you enjoy. Add in the right clothes and shoes to ensure comfort. You can lose weight while having fun.

4. **Reward yourself:** Soak yourself in the post-workout happy feeling, which will motivate you to come back the next day with better enthusiasm. You can also reward yourself with physical presents like buying that pair of quirky shoes you have been eyeing for a while now.

5. **Please do not overdo it:** It is very easy to strain your muscles by overdoing it. It

is essential to take breaks once in a while but restrict it to a concise duration as it can kill the flow and you will have to deal with the burden and stress of starting all over again. Above all, make sure to stay hydrated and eat well.

Undoubtedly, you may have experienced moments when you began a workout routine only to revert to your old habits the very next day. The rigorous exercise programs we vow to adhere to frequently become neglected and abandoned midway. We often prioritize that additional hour of sleep in the morning. So, how do we address this issue? The fundamental approach is to initiate small changes and acknowledge your progress with each incremental step. Let's explore effective call-to-action strategies for incorporating exercise into our daily routines.

Call to Action

Activity 1

Purpose: Guide readers in incorporating brief, restorative breaks into their daily routines.

Instructions

1. Integrate 2-minute breaks into your work and home schedule. These pauses will promote healthy blood circulation, particularly if you spend extended periods in a specific position.

2. Enjoy a leisurely walk around your neighborhood or through your favorite park. This light exercise will invigorate your body and rejuvenate your mind, helping to alleviate fatigue.

3. Please select your favorite song, play it on a loop, and dance to the rhythm. Stay active while enjoying a fun-filled break.

4. Kickstart your day with a preferred exercise routine. Aim for at least ten minutes daily to establish a consistent habit.

Activity 2
Purpose: Cultivate a Daily Exercise Habit
Instructions

1. Partner with a friend or family member who can join your exercise routine or hold you accountable. Having an accountability partner often makes it easier to stay consistent.
2. Begin with manageable activities. Start at home by stretching, walking, or jogging around your living space.
3. Document your objectives to maintain consistency in your routine. Strategize and follow through with your plans.
4. Incrementally extend your exercise sessions by adding an extra ten minutes every week. Gradually push your limits and intensify your workouts.

5. Make mindful food choices by evaluating your calorie intake, as this can significantly impact your overall health and fitness efforts.

6. Prioritize hydration and consider rewarding yourself for pushing boundaries in a healthy way—such as by engaging in a relaxing activity or treating yourself to a non-food-related indulgence.

Activity 3
Purpose: Envision an Improved Version of Yourself
Instructions

1. Describe the goals you plan to accomplish and the desired results that will emerge when exercise becomes a regular part of your life.

2. Consider your progress toward your objectives through consistent daily action, and envision the emotions associated with achieving those outcomes.

Chapter Takeaways

- In this chapter we learned that incorporating a few minutes of regular exercise and self-care practices has been shown to positively impact mental health by reducing stress, anxiety, and depression and promoting overall emotional well-being.

- Regular exercise can have numerous benefits, such as promoting relaxation, boosting energy levels, improving sleep quality, and enhancing self-confidence.

- Physical activities release feel-good endorphins, which are naturally occurring brain chemicals that resemble those found in cannabis. They have been found to boost mood.

- Begin with simple exercises such as stretching, jumping jacks, or a brisk walk for five minutes each day to boost your energy and sustain it throughout the day. It is essential to avoid overexertion and take care of your body by drinking enough water and consuming adequate protein.

- To incorporate exercise routines into your daily life, consider these tips: adjust your viewpoint, focus on commitment, seek pleasure in workouts, reward yourself, and prevent excessive strain.

Embark on a journey towards a healthier, happier you by incorporating exercise into your daily life. I invite you to join the Habits4Miracles Facebook page to share your success stories and inspire others on their wellness journey. Together, we can create a supportive and motivating community, encouraging one another to embrace a more active and fulfilling lifestyle. Take the first step today and inspire others to join you in pursuing health and happiness!

"We need to find our Creator, and that cannot be found in noise and restlessness. Our (Creator) is the friend of silence. See how nature – trees, flowers, grass – grows in silence; see the stars, the moon, the sun, how they move in silence. We need silence to be able to touch souls." - Mother Teresa

CHAPTER 8

The Music in S̲ *"Silence"*

When was the last time you just sat by yourself, not distracted by your thoughts or technology, and truly enjoyed your own company?

If you have difficulty recalling such an occasion, you might need to change things a little in your current lifestyle. Why? Well, one's lifestyle has grown so ingrained with noise that it has been challenging to achieve the golden silence.

Considering how overwhelming our society is sometimes, it is no surprise that many of us struggle to be consistently productive because we keep losing focus. Given all the distractions in our daily lives, we need to surround ourselves with silence to retain our attention and find our inner voice. The problem is that most are led to believe silence is deadly; therefore, they run from it instead of running to it. On the contrary, silence can be a source of healing and restoration.

We are constantly exposed to different types of noise in our everyday lives, whether it be the rumbling of trains passing by, the constant honking of cars in traffic, music blasting from loudspeakers, or people talking on their cell phones. Even though we may try to block out these sounds, they still manage to penetrate our surroundings, adding to the stress and chaos of our daily routine.

Furthermore, the noise in our heads, such as overthinking or worrying, can also be overwhelming and add to our overall stress levels. Finding peace and quiet amidst all the external and internal noise can be difficult. This is especially true when we are trying to focus on important tasks, such as work or studying for exams.

While it may seem like we are unable to escape the constant noise and chaos, there are steps we can take to mitigate its effects on our mental health. This can involve finding quiet spaces to take a break, practicing mindfulness or meditation techniques, and limiting exposure to loud and stressful environments as much as possible. By taking these steps, we can give ourselves the mental and emotional space to recharge and better cope with the noise and stress in our lives.

According to many studies, the average person's brain processes between 60,000 and 80,000 thoughts daily. That is a lot of noise. The modern mind is constantly stimulated, and we are frantically trying to keep up with the amount of data being fed to our brains. So, it's more crucial than ever to pause and appreciate the silence whenever possible. In fact, it's a necessity. In the modern world, we primarily communicate via text and email rather than making phone calls. It is effective for many people but does not convey one's most real emotions, especially when addressing a delicate issue. The lack of face-to-face communication often always leads to miscommunication.

Think of a challenging situation you've faced where your response via email or text made it worse due to your lack of composure. By taking a moment to reflect on the situation and reviewing the message in your drafts folder, chances are you would not want to send it in its current form.

Too much stimulation and noise bombarding us nonstop can be utterly stressful. However, deciding how you want to use the silence is vital. It will only worsen matters if you use the quiet time to worry and contemplate, which is what the brain is programmed to do when we are not engaged in any task. Isn't it funny how our minds are programmed to go the route we may be trying to avoid?

Setting aside five to ten minutes daily of uninterrupted silence can considerably benefit our mental and physical well-being. It gives us a chance to reflect, which will help us counteract our bodies' stress response. When we are under pressure, keeping our composure helps in our decision-making. I have experienced this myself.

When you keep your cool, you have a better chance of succeeding both as a leader and a student. When I was a college student, having loads of chores and deadlines to meet, stress would consume me. Later, I understood that the best action in such circumstances was to keep calm. Even when I encountered situations in my professional life for which I had no amicable answer, taking time for myself proved tremendously helpful. In my journey, I have realized that the issues you seek to resolve through verbal conflicts are more easily resolved through calmness.

If you know how to remain silent while you listen more intently, you can make a home for yourself in someone's heart. Practicing silence and listening techniques can make you more confident and respectable at work. Suppose you want to improve your personal or professional life. In that case, silence is a terrific problem-solver that can help you in multiple ways.

There is a story I recently came across that I often share with people while discussing the significance of silence. It is about a college librarian who once misplaced his priceless watch while sorting the books at the end of the day. Although it would have appeared to be a typical watch, it had significant sentimental worth. He spent considerable time looking everywhere amidst the rows of shelves before growing weary. However, the worn-out librarian was determined to find his watch and decided to ask some students for assistance.

In exchange for helping him retrieve his prized watch, he offered a tempting reward. The students rushed and searched every nook and corner of the library possible. Some gave up after a prolonged search. Only a few worn-out kids remained as the number of students searching for the watch eventually reduced.

The librarian eventually lost all hope and called off the search. Right then, another student approached him as he was about to close for the day and asked him to hold off.

The student finally emerged a little while later with the watch. When inquiring how he found the watch, the boy retorted that he simply sat there trying to hear the watch ticking and directed the search toward the sound he could hear more clearly in the absence of noise. What a message! The boy recognized that the crowd leaving was to his benefit, as it subtracted the unnecessary noise so that he could hear the only noise desired – the watch ticking.

When discussing the importance of silence, it would almost be wrong to leave its prominence in Buddhism. Buddhists teach that contemplation is the key to understanding things and that silence is necessary for achieving enlightenment. Through reflection and self-cultivation, completely motionless monks develop their balance and wisdom.

Silence offers our bodies and minds a much-needed respite from the chaos of everyday life and restores and revitalizes our inner selves. Additionally, silence is good for the brain. According to a study, the memory-related area of the brain – known as the hippocampus – may grow new cells after two hours of stillness. While I understand that it is nearly impossible for us to sit still for two hours, I think it would be a great place to start if we could manage five to ten minutes at a time.

According to a 2017 article in the *Harvard Business Review*, recent research shows that taking a break from noise helps the nervous system recover. It also helps maintain energy and trains our minds to be more adaptable and receptive to the complex circumstances many of us now exist, work in, and lead our lives. I have found that maintaining silence is an effective method for controlling my emotions and avoiding engaging in heated arguments. It aids in reducing my rage and enables me to act responsibly. Now let's delve into the benefits of being silent:

- **Improves concentration:** Digressions and tendencies to overthink can be controlled with the help of silence. Instead of 20,000 other things running in the back of your head, you will be able to concentrate more clearly on the task at hand if you practice taking a moment of true silence in your daily life.
- **Fosters creativity:** Some truly transformative ideas are conceived when we sit in silence and let our minds wander into the depths of our imagination. This is because, in

solitude, we can better organize our ideas and shape our dreams.

- **Improves memory:** Sitting quietly for ten to fifteen minutes can improve memory. Those with amnesia and some forms of dementia may awaken a dormant ability for memory and learn by sitting in silence. The unique memory-enhancing advantages of silent reflection also have promising implications for those with neurological injuries, such as seizures.

- **Improves decision-making:** Making decisions in a loud place is challenging because your brain is constantly overloaded with stimuli. However, even five minutes of stillness decreases the amygdala's stress response and releases the "happy hormones" of serotonin, endorphin, and oxytocin. Your health returns as a result, and your mind becomes more tranquil. You can then process information with clarity and awareness to make better decisions.

Silence can be as rejuvenating to your mind and heart as a stroll through the park, a cup of your favorite coffee in bed, or a night of sound sleep. So go ahead, put your phone away, take a break, and let your body soak in the music of silence. Now that we know the benefits of silence, I am sure you must be looking forward to practicing silence in your daily life. But how do we go about it? Check out our *call-to-action* list to help you get started.

Spend a minimum of thirty minutes daily practicing stillness. However, start small with five or ten minutes of silence, to begin with. Build on the momentum as you start to experience the advantages of this brief time spent in silence and solitude.

To help you through your journey, here are three activities. As you get comfortable with the first activity, move to the second one and strive to make them a part of your daily life.

Call to Action

Activity 1
Purpose: To help readers practice silence.
Instructions

1. Prepare yourself and set yourself to practice five or ten minutes of silence right this moment.

2. Light a candle if you feel it would set the atmosphere.

3. Relax and sit comfortably. Stay present while you listen.

4. Breathe slowly and mindfully, taking in the silence and letting go of mental "noise."

5. At the end of the activity, practice gratitude and positive mind talk.

Activity 2
Purpose: Activities to develop the everyday practice of silence.

Instructions

1. Plan at least two brief moments, ten minutes each, of deliberate stillness each day. Do one before you leave the house in the morning and one after you get home in the evenings. If you are working from home practice it before and after your work hours.

2. Reduce the amount of time you spend using gadgets. You can put your gadgets on silent at certain times in the day to achieve this. If you need a nudge to remind yourself, fall back to your good old alarm clock.

3. When you feel compelled to speak, opt to remain silent. For this, shift your attention to your breath and take a mental note of the things surrounding you. Your silence will grow louder the more you listen to it. This can significantly lessen internal noise and the emotional roller coaster it causes in your brain.

4. Before you say something, think about what you are going to say and why. Always be mindful of your words and the reasons behind them. Evaluate its necessity by asking yourself if it is essential to say something.

Activity 3
Purpose: How to master the art of silence?
Instructions

1. Practice thinking about things before you even say them
2. Avoid interrupting people.
3. Let the other person speak first and be a better listener than a talker; remember, God has given us two ears and only one mouth.

Chapter Takeaways

- We are always glued to our phones as technology continues to dominate our lives. Although we are unaware of it, it negatively impacts our mental health.
- Spending time alone and in silence allows your brain to process your emotions rather than suppressing them.
- You can think clearly, making more informed and strategic decisions that enhance your life when there is silence.

- Silence serves as a sanctuary for our bodies and minds, offering a much-needed break from the constant clamor of daily life, and revitalizing our inner selves. It brings the following benefits: Enhances concentration, Nurtures creativity, Boosts memory, Improves decision-making.

- Start with five to ten minutes of silence each day and build on the momentum as you move forward by committing thirty minutes or more every day. The advantages of it will soon become apparent.

SCAN ME   Discover the profound impact of silence on your personal growth by incorporating it into your daily routine. I invite you to join the Habits4Miracles Facebook page and share your strategies for practicing silence, inspiring others to embrace this powerful tool for self-development. By fostering a supportive community, we can raise awareness of the transformative power of silence and learn from one another's experiences.

"We are the sum of our actions, and therefore our habits make all the difference." - Aristotle

CONCLUSION

The Totality of *M.I.R.A.C.L.E.S.*

Realizing who you desire to be and taking baby steps to form new habits will help you live a healthy and fulfilling life. In the M.I.R.A.C.L.E.S. chapters, we discussed why creating positive habits and their benefits is crucial. Still, the road to developing new and healthy habits is going to be a difficult journey since there will be times when you forget or feel too lazy to practice your new habits.

However, it is crucial to realize that adopting MIRACLES habits will change your thinking and life. I have already explained how to make these small changes in your life with targeted tools and strategies that you can use to develop your habits.

The process works whether you are looking for a life-work balance or seeking peace in your daily life. If you simply want to stop drinking, desire to get in and stay in shape, manage your stress better, or prosper in life in general, these habits are beneficial.

In the first chapter, we looked at what mind-talk entails and ways for its practical application in everyday life. We discussed that positive mind-talk is the primary factor that separates success from failure; thus, cultivating a habit of positive mind-talk helps rewire your brain to maintain happiness.

Behaviors turn into automatic responses through the process of habit formation. Either way, it can happen accidentally or on purpose. Researchers from University College London discovered in a 2009 study that it typically takes 66 days for a behavioral modification to become natural. A significant factor in how long it takes to instill a habit depends on the habit you choose.

Habit formation can take anywhere from eighteen to two-hundred and fifty-four days because some habits are more challenging to acquire than others.

In the second chapter, we discussed ideation and the various methods for generating unique and original ideas regularly. To foster creativity and a profusion of ideas, we also looked at strategies to combat the propensity of forgetting these thoughts and ideas as they come to us.

Calls to action at the end of each chapter ensure you can hop on the bandwagon of making small changes in real-time as you read the book. It's important to understand that you will be waiting a very long time if you wait for things to be perfect to start working on things because there is no ideal time than RIGHT NOW.

There will always be something amiss or a feeling there will be a better time. But honestly, there is never a perfect time. As you go along, you can make changes, and things change only when you act right away.

The third chapter discussed how reading is essential and improves your knowledge, sensitivity, and creative thinking skills. Likewise, it might also help in just winding down following a tiring day at work or school. We also looked at how we may improve interactions and relationships at work by fostering reading habits.

In Chapter Four, we delved into the significance of analyzing our thoughts and behaviors as a crucial step towards personal development. By taking the time to reflect on our past actions, we can learn from them and build a better future for ourselves. However, it's important not to get caught up in over-analyzing situations, as this can lead to analytical paralysis, where we become stuck in a cycle of overthinking and indecision.

It's also essential not to get bogged down by the imperfections of our circumstances. We mustn't waste time doubting ourselves, our abilities, or the amount of time we have available to make positive changes in our lives. Instead, we must focus on taking action towards our goals and instilling better habits in our lifestyle.

Remember that progress, not perfection, is the key to success. Don't get caught up in striving for an unattainable standard of perfection. Instead, focus on making small, consistent steps towards your goals, and don't let setbacks or mistakes discourage you from continuing to move forward.

By embracing the process of analysis without getting caught up in overthinking and self-doubt, we can unlock our potential and achieve our personal development goals. So, take the time to reflect, learn from your experiences, and move forward with confidence, knowing that every step you take is bringing you closer to your desired outcome.

Chapter five examines the importance of remaining composed because it helps you focus on and finish your work more quickly. You can improve your ability to maintain composure at work by exercising or taking a short stroll each day. Additionally, by developing mental calmness, you can strengthen your inner self and rely less and less on other forces. Even though everyone gets irritated, and anger is a common emotion, it is crucial to learn how to regulate it. As discussed, "Faking Calm" is an excellent technique for improved emotional regulation. Your inner voice is your intrinsic knowledge.

Chapter six highlights the importance of listening to your inner voice as a valuable resource when seeking guidance or advice. Our inner voice can provide insights into our thoughts, feelings, and values and help us make more informed decisions. Journaling and walking are two effective ways to clear mental fog and tap into our inner voice. By taking time to reflect through journaling, we can gain clarity and perspective on our experiences and emotions. Walking can also serve as meditative practice, allowing us to clear our minds and focus on the present moment. Both journaling and walking can help us connect with our inner selves and strengthen our intuition, which can be a valuable tool in decision-making and problem-solving. By practicing self-reflection and mindfulness, we can cultivate a deeper understanding of ourselves and our needs and lead a more fulfilling and purposeful life.

Chapter Seven emphasizes the benefits of incorporating physical exercise into our daily routine. Regular physical activity has been proven to have positive effects on mental health, cardiovascular health, and cognitive function. We can improve our overall well-being and quality of life by engaging in just a few minutes of exercise each day.

Physical exercise can have a profound impact on our mental health by reducing stress, anxiety, and depression. Exercise releases endorphins, which are natural chemicals in the brain that promote feelings of happiness and well-being. Exercise can also improve our cardiovascular health, by reducing the risk of heart disease, stroke, and other chronic conditions.

In addition to mental and cardiovascular benefits, physical exercise has also been shown to improve cognitive function, such as memory, attention, and learning. Exercise stimulates the growth of new brain cells and strengthens the connections between existing cells.

Incorporating physical exercise into our daily routine doesn't have to be time-consuming or difficult. Even a few minutes of exercise, such as taking a brisk walk, doing some stretching or yoga, or practicing bodyweight exercises, can have a significant impact on our overall health and well-being. By prioritizing physical activity, we can reap the numerous benefits that exercise has to offer.

Chapter eight emphasizes the significance of finding moments of silence and solitude amidst our busy lives. Taking just a few minutes each day to be alone with our thoughts and feelings can help us better process and navigate life's challenges. Incorporating practices such as meditation, journaling, or simply sitting in quiet contemplation can have profound benefits for our mental and emotional health.

In today's fast-paced world, we are bombarded with constant stimulation and distractions. Finding moments of silence can help us recharge and renew our energy, enabling us to be more present and effective in our daily lives. By disconnecting from external stimuli and turning inward, we can cultivate a deeper sense of self-awareness and inner peace.

Incorporating silence and solitude into our daily routine doesn't have to be time-consuming or complicated. Even just ten minutes of quiet reflection can provide significant benefits. Engaging in practices like meditation, journaling, or nature walks can help us develop greater mindfulness, clarity, and emotional resilience. By prioritizing moments of silence and solitude, we can cultivate a more centered and grounded sense of self, and better navigate the challenges and opportunities that come our way.

The core reality is that implementing one habit at a time is a more feasible and sustainable approach than attempting to incorporate all of our desired habits at once. Focusing on one habit at a time can establish a solid foundation and build momentum toward achieving our goals. This approach allows us to develop new habits gradually and with greater intentionality rather than feeling overwhelmed or discouraged by trying to do too much too soon.

The book's call to action activities after each chapter are designed to be accessible and practical for readers to implement as they read. By incorporating small, manageable changes into our daily routine, we can start to build a foundation for lasting positive change. The calls to action are designed to encourage readers to take action and apply the concepts and strategies discussed in the book to their own lives.

By focusing on one habit at a time and implementing the practical strategies provided in the book, readers can achieve meaningful and lasting change in their lives.

Finally, I encourage readers to visit the book's Facebook page to share experiences: https://www.facebook.com/Habits4MIRAC LES. By openly sharing our journey of implementing new habits, we can inspire and support each other towards personal growth and transformation.

With a heartfelt invitation, I encourage you to join the Habits4Miracles Facebook page and become part of a community dedicated to fostering positivity and personal development. This uplifting space allows us to work together to empower one another, revealing our true potential and experiencing incredible results. By sharing our individual journeys, insights, and support, we can help each other build lives that align with our distinct aspirations and ambitions. Seize the chance to contribute to a collective journey of self-betterment, and together, let's create a brighter future for ourselves and those around us. Thank you for your time and effort in reading Habits4Miracles and for sharing its positive influence on your life.

ABOUT THE AUTHOR

Meet Rahul Karan Sharma, a remarkable individual who kindles the flame of inspiration and epitomizes authentic leadership. His life's purpose is to empower others to unleash their boundless potential and foster positive transformations in their lives. Driven by unwavering determination and a relentless pursuit of excellence, Rahul has emerged as a distinguished author, mesmerizing public speaker, and life-changing coach, captivating hearts and minds worldwide with his zeal for personal growth and self-improvement. His inspiration is rooted in his father's quote, "Where there is a will, there is a way."

Rahul's conviction that a single shift in mindset can be a game-changer has made him a faithful advocate of lifelong learning. With an MBA in Human Resources from Pune University and a Master's degree in Organization Development from Bowling Green State University, Rahul's academic accomplishments is a testament to his dedication to personal growth and the pursuit of excellence.

Originating from Ujjain, India, and completing his high school education at The Daly College in Indore, Rahul cultivated a profound appreciation for independence, discipline, and sportsmanship through his involvement with the National Cadet Corp and Cricket Academy. Leveraging his innate storytelling prowess and in-depth knowledge of organizational dynamics, Rahul enables individuals and teams to actualize their highest potential.

Rahul's literary creations, such as "Habits4Miracles" and the best-selling new release "Be Action Oriented," offer invaluable insights that enable individuals to carve their careers into extraordinary journeys.

Rahul's dedication to servant leadership has touched countless lives. With years of experience in the field, he has mastered the art of building high-performing teams and nurturing leaders. Anchored in the belief that leaders can be cultivated through effective coaching and mentorship, Rahul passionately devotes himself to unlocking the potential within individuals and teams.

Residing in Ashburn, Virginia, Rahul shares his life with his lovely wife and their two endearing children, creating a warm, nurturing home environment filled with love and joy. In his treasured leisure moments, Rahul delights in spending quality time with his loved ones, exploring the intricacies of his mind with a game of Sudoku, and revitalizing his body through swimming. His insatiable thirst for knowledge propels him to continually seek innovative ways to learn and evolve personally and professionally.

SCAN ME Thank you for joining me on the journey of personal growth. I cordially invite you to follow me on social media, where we can continue to exchange our experiences, insights, and enthusiasm for self-improvement. By collaborating, we can cultivate a caring and supportive community, encouraging each other as we strive to reach our full potential. Let's stay in touch and spread kindness and optimism, motivating one another every step of the way.